EVANGELISTIC

PROGRAM BUILDER
No. 2

Compiled by Paul M. Miller

Lillenas Publishing Company
Kansas City, MO 64141

Cover art by Art Jacobs

Contents

Everlasting King

Just and true in all His ways.
Eternally the same.
Saving all who call on Him.
Unlocking every chain.
Showing light unto the blind.

Caring for the soul.
Having great compassion.
Reaching down to those below.
Inviting whomsoever will, into His home above.
Sharing life, by giving life.
Teaching all to love.

—Gena E. Owens

One Reason

I trip and I fall and so skin up my soul;
Bruising my heart, my falls take their toll.
Bleeding from wounds where healing is slow . . .
But, knowing the scars will cause me to grow.
My life with its little tumbles and trips
Can leave this man's spirit tattered with rips.
But, the Healer awaits to respond when I call,
A Friend stands alert to help when I fall . . .
He's Jesus, sweet Jesus, the Son of the Father.
He's never too busy, and I'm never a bother;
He comes to my aid and mends with His touch,
And this is one reason I love Him so much.

—Dave Eales

He Cares for Them

Are we more than they that we should claim
   Christ's love as ours alone?
He said, "Whosoever will may come";
   Are some hearts made of stone?

Are we such a special love of God's
   His mercy, oh, so small?
Is there not enough to go around?
   God's grace was meant for all.

Are we made of so much finer clay
   We cannot feel their need?
Is heaven for us and not for them?
   Oh, why not say, "Lord, lead!"

He cares for them! Christ cares for them!
   His love is full and free;
Christ cares for them—the other ones—
   The same as you and me.

—Phyllis C. Michael

Blind Faith

Wretched beggar, Bartimaeus,
   Crouching in eternal night,
Have you heard the Master's coming?
   Jesus Christ, the Son of Light.

Sightless eyes are lifted, searching,
   From his lips there falls a plea,
O Thou blessed Son of David,
   Grant Your mercy unto me.

"Hush, you beggar," shout the watchers,
   "Jesus has no time for thee."
All the more they heard him crying,
   "Jesus, Lord, come rescue me."

In the pathway Jesus halted,
   Ears attuned to mercy's cry,
"Rise and come, blind Bartimaeus,
   For I cannot pass you by."

Tearing off the ragged garment,
  Derilect boldly makes his way
Sightless eyes, by faith were seeing,
  Though they knew no light of day.

"What would'st thou?" the Savior bid him,
  "What blessing can I work for you?"
"To see, to see," the beggar answered,
  "That my eyes may be as new."

"Go thy way," the Master bid him,
  "Walk no more in shades of night.
I, the Lord, can grant your healing,
  Your 'blind faith' has granted sight."

—Lowell Long

I'll Go

(May be used as a song or words only. May be used as recitation with several children reciting the chorus together after verse 4.)

Was it for this my Savior came?
  For this He bore my sin and shame
That some should die in darkest night,
  Nor ever breathe His precious name?

CHORUS:

For this? For this? Oh, no, Lord, no!
I'll take my cross and follow Thee;
I've heard Thy voice, I've made my choice,
O precious Lord, I'll go! I'll go!

Was it for this Christ left His throne?
  For this He felt He must atone?
That I should wait thus idly by,
  And let Him bear the Cross alone?

Was it for this my Savior died?
  For this my Lord was crucified?
That Satan's power should rule the world,
  Because I, too, His love denied?

Was it for this Christ set us free?
  For this He bled on Calvary's tree?
A world enslaved by greed and fear;
  Consumed by hate from sea to sea?

—Phyllis C. Michael

7

Fishers of Men

by Martha Bolton

Characters:
> SAM
> BILL

(Scene opens with SAM *in his garage or workroom, repairing a few items.* BILL *approaches.)*

BILL: Hi, Sam. What are you doing?

SAM: Just repairing a few things. The grandkids were up last weekend!

BILL: I know what you mean. Mine are the same way. I still haven't repaired the garage door from their last visit!

SAM: What did they do, break it?

BILL: No! They took it off! *(Pause)* It's my own fault, I guess. I bought them one of those toy tool sets for Christmas.

SAM *(laughs):* But you wouldn't trade them for all the money in the world, right?

BILL: Oh, I don't know. Make me an offer! *(Both laugh)* . . . How about doing a little fishing tomorrow morning?

SAM *(shakes head):* By the time I get home from church, I don't think the fish will be biting.

BILL: Then don't go to church . . . I'll even buy the bait!

SAM: Now that's an offer I don't get every day! But I'm afraid I'll have to pass this time, Bill.

BILL: I don't give rain checks . . .

SAM *(laughs):* I know, but thanks anyway.

BILL: You really believe in all that religious stuff?

SAM: You mean God?

BILL: God . . . church . . . "Amazing Grace" . . . all of it. . . . You really buy it, huh?

SAM: Bill, today the Word of God is the only thing we can believe in.

BILL: But it's outdated. We're into computers, not sheep. We travel in spaceships, not arks.

SAM: The Bible is as relevant today as it was when it was written. You want to hand me that hammer over there?

BILL *(gets hammer and gives it to* SAM): Boy *(looking over broken table)*, your grandkids sure did a number on this table.

SAM: My wife broke that one. It's just in line to be fixed.

BILL: So you really believe in the Ten Commandments and all that?

SAM: If you think about it, Bill, most of our laws are rooted in the Ten Commandments.

BILL: And you believe in loving your neighbor as yourself?

SAM: It's one of the greatest commandments.

BILL: Then can I borrow your fishing pole? You won't be needing it at church.

SAM *(laughs):* Now that was sure sneaky! Sure, it's right over there leaning against the wall.

BILL *(goes over to get it):* Sam, this is your last chance . . . are you sure you don't want to go?

SAM: I'm sure.

BILL: You know, Sam, I just can't figure you out. Every Sunday you get up and go to church just to sit in an old pew while every Sunday I'm out there on the river, fishing and relaxing. Now you tell me who's got the better life.

SAM: I don't know, Bill. Why don't you tell me.

BILL: All I know is when I'm fishing, I don't worry about anything. I have no problems, no headaches, everything's peaceful.

SAM: And what happens when you dock the boat and hang up the fishing pole? What about Monday . . . and Tuesday . . . and the rest of the week? How do you handle your problems then? Do you take off and go fishing again?

BILL: No, but sometimes I'd like to.

SAM: Well, Bill, my peace stays with me throughout the whole week. Jesus gives me a joy the world can't take away. It's just as real on a boat fishing as it is at home paying bills. So, Bill, you tell me, who's got the better life?

(BILL *looks at fishing pole . . . hands it back to* SAM.)

BILL: What time's church?

SAM: I'll pick you up at 9:30.

BILL: We'll go fishing Monday morning. Anyway, everyone knows fish bite better on weekdays!

The Reunion

by Carolyn Rathbun

Characters:
　　PAT: mother and homemaker, a growing Christian
　　CAROLYN: Pat's sister, rich and restless
　　BOB: Pat's husband, also a growing Christian

Props:
　　Chairs or a couch center stage.
　　Two exits are needed.

(CAROLYN *enters* PAT's *living room [through doorway 1] and* PAT *rushes to hug her.* CAROLYN *remains distant, even in the embrace.)*

PAT: Oh, Carolyn, I'm so glad to see you again!

CAROLYN: Yes, it has been a long time, hasn't it? *(Disengages herself)*

PAT: How was your trip?

CAROLYN: Fine, Pat.

PAT: We'll have to tell each other everything that's happened since you left!

CAROLYN: Of course.

(Several moments of uncomfortable silence pass, with PAT *searching for a way to begin and* CAROLYN *moving restlessly around the room.)*

PAT: Your life must be so exciting—traveling in all those foreign countries with Barnett.

CAROLYN: Oh, yes, marvelous, dear. I must tell you about it. But, how is your husband, and your children?

PAT *(joyfully):* They're healthy and sweet. We're very happy.

CAROLYN *(disdainfully):* But is . . . Bob . . . still, you know . . . doing the same job?

PAT: Uh-huh. Still a trash collector. He loves the outdoor work, you know, and he has some close friends in the company. He's had good experiences working there.

CAROLYN: Hmmph! I wonder at a sister of mine who can be mindlessly happy with a . . . a garbage man!

11

(PAT *never stops smiling, but her eyes sadden.*)

PAT: I am happy, Carolyn.

CAROLYN: Well, enough of this commiserating. We have a lot of catching up to do. You were good enough to write and keep me up on your family news. I'm afraid writing is not my strong suit.

PAT: There are things I wanted to tell you face-to-face too.

CAROLYN *(preoccupied with fingernails):* Oh? And I'm sure I have loads to tell you about these past six years.

PAT: One thing is really more recent, only about the last two years or so.

CAROLYN: Don't tell me! You've finally finished college? Or started a career?

PAT: No, nothing like that. I'm satisfied with my work here.

CAROLYN *(shaking her head):* I don't understand how you can be excited about that . . . now, I think there's nothing more exciting than going to a gala dinner party for a duke or a sheikh, with all the glitter and glamour that accompanies it. You poor thing, you'll never know the romance of that. Or the excitement of opening night on Broadway. You know, I even watched part of the Irish war from the windows of a suite in Dublin one evening!

PAT: Mmm. Are you happy?

CAROLYN: Happy? Of course! I mean, who wouldn't be happy, with all the money one wants, and travel, and social standing. Naturally, I'm happy.

PAT: Oh.

CAROLYN *(harshly):* What is that supposed to mean, "Oh"?

PAT: Nothing. You just don't seem very happy.

CAROLYN: Just tired, that's all. *(Impatiently)* Now, what was it you were going to tell me, dear?

PAT: I'm not sure . . . well, I've waited all this time to tell you, so I guess I better go ahead.

CAROLYN: Yes, do.

(PAT *moves around room as she shares.* CAROLYN *sits on couch but acts restless and disinterested.*)

PAT: You know Thad, my second boy?

CAROLYN: Thad, Thad. How old is he?

PAT: He's six now, but when this happened he was only four.

CAROLYN: What about him?

PAT: Thad has always liked climbing. I had warned him that our old apple tree would not hold him, but he didn't pay any attention. I could have spanked him for it a hundred times, but his love for the sky kept him going back up.

CAROLYN: Yes, yes.

PAT: One morning I was dressing Terry, the baby, when my oldest boy raced into the room screaming, "Thad's fallen out of the tree!" When I ran out, there was our Thad, lying still and white. He looked dead. I must have screamed . . . several of the neighbors hurried out and took over. One covered Thad with a blanket; she said he was still breathing. Another neighbor called Bob and an ambulance . . . *(Lost in remembering)*

CAROLYN: What then?

PAT: All the way to the hospital in the ambulance I was crying and praying. I hadn't prayed for a long, long time. But when I was faced with the death of my son, I turned back to God.

CAROLYN: Mm.

PAT: Well, I prayed through that day and night, but my prayers were demanding, accusing. "Why me, God, why us?" Thad got worse. His kidneys failed, and he had internal bleeding. He was dying. I didn't want to give him up. I was angry. Even Bob couldn't get through to me. I kept badgering God, trying to force a blessing from Him.

CAROLYN: Go on.

PAT: Finally, my tears were all dried up. Fear and hurt were constantly in my heart. I looked out the hospital window and tried to think clearly. I thought, Well, if God wants Thad, he'd be much happier there anyway. I'll just have to let him go. So out loud I said, "OK, God, I'm tired of fighting You. If You want him, he's Yours. I'm willing to let him go to You."

(CAROLYN *has ceased fidgeting and begins to be interested, in spite of herself.)*

CAROLYN: Did anything happen? Anything change?

PAT: Yes, something changed. Me! Suddenly I had peace inside, and I knew I had done the right thing. The Lord gave me peace in place of the fear, and joy in place of the hurt. I still didn't know whether Thad would live or not, though.

CAROLYN: What then?

PAT: I turned away from the window and standing at the side of Thad's bed was an angel.

CAROLYN: You're kidding!

PAT: No, Carolyn, I saw him. I can't deny it. He didn't even look toward me, but he gazed very lovingly down at Thad. He put his hands on Thad's head for a few moments, then he was gone. Just like that!

CAROLYN: I assume Thad got better.

PAT: He slept peacefully through the night, and in three days he came home. He'd been completely healed!

CAROLYN: Come on!

PAT: Carolyn, it's all true. It really happened.

CAROLYN *(bitterly):* Maybe God, if He's real, does love children. Maybe. But that's the end of it. They grow up into adults. I'm sure He's done with us then.

PAT: That's not true!

CAROLYN: Oh, yes, little sister. You haven't seen the world as I have seen it. There's too much filth and ugliness for God to love it.

PAT *(sadly):* I'm sorry you feel that way.

CAROLYN *(abruptly):* Well! I'm glad Thad is well. I should tell you about the shah's third wife . . . Why should I? I'm tired of that story.

PAT: Carolyn, there's a story I could tell you that I never get tired of.

CAROLYN: You've overpowered me with your stories already, Sis.

(They pass a few moments in silence, PAT *calm and* CAROLYN *nervous.)*

CAROLYN *(abruptly):* Just tell me one thing! WHAT IS IT YOU HAVE? Why are you so happy to live with a garbage collector and three little brats? WHAT IS IT?

PAT: Carolyn, it's . . .

CAROLYN: I mean, *I* should be the happy one—with a fortune to spend every day of my life, and a husband who loves me, if he loves anyone. And I still have a restlessness . . . as if I don't have it all. So what do you have that I don't have?

PAT: Jesus Christ.

CAROLYN *(harshly):* Don't give me that. I tried religion, just like you, when we were young and foolish.

PAT: But we never tried Jesus.

CAROLYN: Besides, I'm a good woman. I don't murder, steal, or lie, or any of that kind of . . .

PAT: That's not enough!

CAROLYN: It was enough for Moses!

PAT: But, Carolyn, if you love money and things more than God, your heart is just not in the right place!

CAROLYN: And where do you get off telling me where my heart is! Sure, I like having all the money I want—and if you think I'll give that up, you're crazy!

PAT *(tenderly):* No, I can't say you have to give up your money. I think you might have to give up worshiping it, though.

CAROLYN: Forget it, Sis. Nothing is worth that.

(CAROLYN *haughtily exits door 2.)*

PAT: Carolyn! Oh, dear. Praise the Lord!

(Offstage voice of BOB *is heard, then he enters by door 1.)*

BOB: Pat, are you here, Honey?

PAT: In here, Sweetheart. *(Gives* BOB *a big hug)*

BOB: Well, where's Carolyn?

PAT: She's out on the back porch. I think she'll be back in a minute or two.

BOB: Have you had a chance to tell her?

PAT: Oh, yes. I just hope I didn't go overboard too early!

BOB: How did she react?

PAT: Well, basically, she gave the "rich young ruler" reply, but . . .

BOB: But what?

PAT: Jesus only had one chance with him, and I have three more days.

BOB: What do you think are the chances that she'll listen?

PAT: In my prayers for her, the Lord has given me a great hope. I'll keep that hope for her. I've claimed her for Him, but even if I don't get to see the fruit of that claim, I'm sure it's valid. His promises never fail, right?

BOB: No, Honey, they never do! Praise the Lord!

PAT: Well, let's go find her. We still have a lot of catching up to do!

(PAT *and* BOB *exit door 2.*)

Unveiled!

A Readers Theater

by Bette Dale Moore

ONE and THREE are women, TWO and FOUR are men.

ONE: "As the deer pants for streams of water, so my soul pants for you, O God.

TWO: "My soul thirsts for God, for the living God.

THREE: "When can I go and meet with God?

FOUR: "My tears have been my food day and night,

ONE & THREE: "while men say to me all day long,

TWO & FOUR: "'Where is your God?'

(Slight pause)

ONE: "Why are you downcast, O my soul?

TWO: "Why so disturbed within me?

THREE: "Put your hope in God,

FOUR: "For I will yet praise him,

ALL: "My Savior and my God" (Psalm 42:1-3, 5, NIV).

(Pause)

TWO: I wish it was as simple as that.

ONE: What?

TWO: Oh! You know, the Psalmist's cure for mankind's eternal spiritual quest—simply trust in Someone bigger than yourself.

THREE: You sound skeptical. Don't you believe in God?

TWO: I suppose I do, after a fashion. But I also believe in depression.

FOUR *(puzzled):* Depression?

TWO: Yes. That's what I end up with every time I start getting religious.

ONE: Then, perhaps you need a little less "religion" . . .

17

THREE: . . . and a little more knowledge of God himself.

TWO: Perhaps. How would you describe God?

ONE: The Creator.

THREE: The Supreme Being.

FOUR: The Almighty Father.

ONE: Omniscient.

THREE: Omnipotent.

FOUR: Omnipresent.

TWO *(glumly; speaks in low tones):* Ominous.

ONE, THREE, FOUR *(together):* Ominous?

TWO: Definitely. Look, I try to live a good life; I really do! But I'm certainly not perfect. A God who knows everything, has absolute power, and is everywhere at once has got to spell big trouble for me.

FOUR *(brisk, businesslike):* Date . . .

(THREE *gives the actual date of the performance.)*

FOUR: Time . . .

(THREE *gives the time.)*

FOUR: Category . . .

THREE: Commission, and/or omission.

FOUR *(looks at* THREE, *somewhat exasperated):* Well, which is it? I can't put it down as both.

THREE *(flustered):* I don't know. It's hard to say.

FOUR: Not again. *(Sighs)* Which does he have the most of?

THREE: Um . . . it looks like "Omission" has a slight lead.

FOUR: OK, I'll put it under "Commission" then. *(Businesslike again)* Specific sin . . .

THREE: Lack of faith.

FOUR: Ah, yes. That's a popular one; but it is hard to categorize. Well, let's go on. *(Businesslike)* Total number of sins . . .

THREE: Six million, three hundred thousand, four hundred ninety-two.

18

(THREE *holds script to one side and looks out and down—as if from heaven to earth.* FOUR *looks with her.*)

THREE: But don't put THE BOOK away yet. It looks like 93 is j-u-s-t about ready to happen.

ONE: Is that what you think God is? Some big "Scorekeeper in the Sky"?

TWO: Well, isn't He?

(FOUR *speaks as a high-energy, D.J. announcer type.*)

FOUR: Of course not. God is much too big to be concerned with our every-day problems and sins. Why do you suppose He gave us a mind with which to reason or the ability to tell right from wrong? It's because He wants us to take care of ourselves!

(FOUR *winks, clicks tongue against roof of mouth twice, and gives "thumbs up" gesture.*)

ONE: Then, what *earthly* good is He?

FOUR *(shocked):* Why, He created the entire universe! That's a big enough contribution from any god, I should think!

THREE: But then, after HE created everything, you say He just went off and left it?

FOUR: Yes, more or less.

ONE: Well, if that's true . . . and God's not even around anymore, how can we ever hope to know Him?

TWO *(frustrated):* But if I can't know Him before I die, how do I know if He's the kind of God that will even let me into heaven?

FOUR: That's the chance we all take, Buddy-Boy! Live a good life and hope for the best.

(FOUR *winks, clicks, and "thumbs up."*)

TWO: Now I'm really depressed.

(THREE *speaks as a whiny, long-suffering character.*)

THREE: Don't listen to him and his "watchmaker's theology." He's all wrong. It is possible to know God. I should know! I put my trust in the Lord 23 years ago . . . and He's never failed me yet. *(Sniffs)* Since that time, God has taken away my job; my beautiful home—*(aside to audience)* a two-story colonial that I poured my very heart and soul into; my lovely fam-ily—*(aside)* you would think they'd have the decency to write their poor old mother every now and then; and yes, even my health—*(aside)* five major surgeries in the past three years *(coughs and sniffs).*

(FOUR *takes out a tissue and holds it in his right hand, toward* THREE. THREE *takes tissue from* FOUR *without looking at him as she begins sobbing.)*

THREE: But don't, I repeat, don't feel sorry for me. It's the cross I gladly bear. And yes, it has been worth it all. I am happy to say *(begins sobbing)* that I am a child of God and I am closer to the Lord now than ever before. *(Sadly)* "The Lord gave and the Lord hath taken away" (Job 1:21).

TWO *(incredulous)*: You say that God is your Father? What kind of a God would treat His own child that way?

ONE: A righteous God!

FOUR: A holy God!

ONE: A just God!

TWO: Aren't you leaving something out? Whatever happened to "a loving God"?

ONE: If God is merely a God of affliction . . .

ONE & TWO: . . . then who needs a devil?

FOUR *(vehemently)*: "My son, despise thou not the chastening of the Lord . . . For whom the Lord loveth he chasteneth, and scourgeth every son whom he receiveth" (Hebrews 12:5-6).

TWO: Oh, great! That's just what I need—a "loving" God that's out to get me. *(Shakes head)* Ominous . . . and *(speaks with low tones directly into microphone)* ominous-er.

ONE: If I were you, I'd stop asking everybody else what God is like. If you really want to know Him, you're going to have to meet Him yourself.

TWO: How? I feel like God is hidden from me behind some mysterious "curtain."

THREE: You're right. He is.

ONE: It's called a "veil." Moses hid his face with one when he first read the Law to the children of Israel.

FOUR: And "to this day the same veil remains when the old covenant is read. It has not been removed" (2 Corinthians 3:14, NIV).

TWO: So, how does a person get beyond the curtain?

FOUR: Simple, stop living in the Old Testament . . .

ONE: . . . and step into the New.

TWO *(frustrated):* How?

THREE: Not "How"? . . .

ONE *(emphatically):* . . . Who?

ONE & THREE: Jesus Christ!

FOUR: For He has ". . . destroyed the barrier,

THREE: ". . . the dividing wall of hostility,

FOUR: ". . . by abolishing in his flesh the law with its commandments and regulations" (Ephesians 2:14-15, NIV).

ONE: And ". . . now a righteousness from God . . .

THREE: ". . . apart from law . . .

FOUR: ". . . comes through faith in Jesus Christ . . .

ONE, THREE & FOUR: ". . . to all who believe" (Romans 3:21-22, NIV).

ONE: Therefore "whenever anyone turns to the Lord, the veil is taken away" (2 Corinthians 3:16, NIV).

TWO: Then, you mean, to know Jesus is to know God?

THREE: Yes! for "He is the image of the invisible God" (Colossians 1:15, NIV). Jesus said:

(FOUR *quotes the following scripture using hand gestures to indicate "me," "Father," and "you" on the last sentence.)*

FOUR: "If you really knew me, you would know my Father as well" (John 14:7, NIV). "He who loves me will be loved by my Father, and I too will love him and show myself to him" (John 14:21, NIV).

TWO: Jesus did not come to attack,

ONE: . . . or abandon,

TWO: . . . or afflict His people.

THREE: While He was here, He forgave,

FOUR: . . . He healed,

THREE: . . . He comforted.

ONE: And "Jesus Christ is the same yesterday and today and forever" (Hebrews 13:8, NIV).

TWO: A friend who answers our call and walks along beside us:

21

THREE: . . . to cheer,

FOUR: . . . to guide,

ONE: . . . to defend.

ALL: The Comforter!

ONE: "Praise be to the God and Father of our Lord Jesus Christ,

TWO: ". . . the Father of compassion,

THREE: ". . . and the God of all comfort" (2 Corinthians 1:3, NIV).

FOUR: "And [now] we, who with unveiled faces all reflect the Lord's glory,

TWO: ". . . are being transformed into his likeness,

FOUR: ". . . with ever-increasing glory" (2 Corinthians 3:18, NIV).

THREE: No longer bound by law;

TWO: . . . we are free in Christ!

THREE: Delivered by grace!

ONE & THREE: We *can* know God;

TWO & FOUR: . . . for we have seen His Son;

ALL: . . . and He is God!

The Traveling Actors
or
The Beggars Scene

by Donald M. Mauck

This scene is one scene in the liturgical drama *The Kingdom,* a play centering on the rite of penance or reconciliation. It can be played as a separate unit. It is suggested that a hymn be included perhaps at the beginning of the play—two verses—and then at the close of the scene. In several productions, the actors have given out bread at the close of the scene, while the hymn is being sung.

Characters:

ONE & TWO are men
THREE & FOUR are women
LEVI

Props:

A coat tree has been used in some productions, down right, as indication of the "tree" that has been climbed by LEVI. This is not necessary. The tree can be entirely imaginary.

A recorder, hand cymbals, and tambourine have been used as the instruments for the actors to use during the singing of the song.

Some kind of bag for TWO to use to carry these instruments is needed.

Setting:

At the beginning of the scene, THREE is on shoulders of TWO, ONE, with FOUR assisting in holding her up to look out "over the tree."

TWO: Did he make it? Did he get in?

FOUR: Did they take him in?

THREE: Don't push so. I'm trying to see what happened.

ONE: Ouch, you're digging into my shoulder, you lout.

THREE: Hold still! Hold still! I can't see when you jiggle so.

ONE: My bad leg. It won't hold much longer.

FOUR: You and your leg. Always complaining.

TWO: Is he in the house? Did he get in through the roof?

THREE: I think so. Yes, he's gone, down through the opening. He's in; crashed to the floor.

TWO: At last!

ONE: Watch out. Grab hold of the tree.

FOUR: Don't let go.

THREE: Hold me, you fools, hold me.

TWO: The branch will break. You'll fall.

ONE: Your foot's in my face. Fool!

FOUR: Don't let her go!

THREE: Hold me, hold me! Owww, I'm coming down.

(She tumbles to the ground and they fall over each other, in a heap.)

TWO: Now you've done it.

FOUR: You did it on purpose, you swine.

THREE: Don't you call me names.

ONE: I'm dead, dead. Owww, my back. My back.

FOUR: It's your leg, remember?

ONE: What do you know? It's my back. Owww, I can't walk.

TWO: Look at your arm. It's probably broken too.

ONE: Yes, yes. Oww, my foot! My foot!

FOUR: Why did you fall? You're so clumsy.

THREE: Why? Because you weren't watching, that's why. And it's such a little tree.

TWO: It got Levi up there. Be glad of that.

FOUR: I knew it was dangerous. She never does anything right.

THREE: I'll scratch your eyes out, you dolt!

(FOUR *and* THREE *rush toward each other, as if to fight, interrupted by* TWO.)

TWO: Shut up, both of you.

ONE: Owww, there's nothing to be done, nothing.

Two: So here we are.

Four: And now we wait.

Three: I don't know why we came. It won't do any good. You'll see.

One: Ow, my head, my head.

Two: All right, all right. That does it. *(Pulls* One *up to his feet)* You're next. Here, up the tree with you. You go tell them your legs are broken, your head's busted, your arms are aching, your back's sprained. Here, go on. May you be healed all the way to hell. *(As they try to boost him, unwillingly, up the tree)*

One: No, no. Not up that tree. I couldn't make it. I'd fall, I tell you. I'm all right.

Four: Yes, you're all right. All you need is a swift kick in the—

One *(as he runs from her):* No, no. Don't hit me. I'll stop. I'll stop. No more complaining.

Two: Ha! Who can believe that?

Three: They wouldn't let you in, anyway. You know that. They all know who you are. They've seen you.

One: Me? And what about you? Do you think it would be any different for the three of you? We've all tried to get in before.

Three: Doors are shut to us.

Four: No one wants us! Especially with her along.

Three: I'll get you, you polecat!

Four: Lizard face!

Two *(between the two of them):* You two never stop, do you?

One: What will happen to Levi? Will the Healer listen to him, put His hands on him?

Three: Who knows? They'll probably boot him right out here.

One: Suppose there's no change, and he still can't walk?

Two: No change? There won't be a change. You know that. It's all a hoax.

Three: Then why did we come? All day we've been carrying him.

Four: And then we had to climb that tree and push him up on the roof. It wasn't easy.

Two: Why? I'll tell you why. Because we're sick and tired of hearing about it. "If only I could go to the Healer, if only . . . if only." It was time to call his bluff, I say.

One: I think it will help. Everyone says . . .

Two: Everyone says. Everyone says. Everyone says . . . tomorrow there will be roses and sweet cakes; tomorrow the Kingdom will come. And look at us. Look at us. Do you believe it?

Three: But if he isn't healed, if he can't walk, then . . .

Two: Then it's the same old story for us: lugging him around from place to place, while we do our act.

Four: I'm tired of it, sick of it. There must be a better way.

Two: Better way? You tell me, when you find it. You looked through the window, didn't you? You saw between the branches. *(He motions up right, through the "tree.")*

Four: Yes, I saw.

Three: And so did I. Why can't we go in?

Four: You? They'd take one look at you and send you spinning.

Two: It isn't for us. They told us that long ago.

Three: We'll show them. We'll show them someday.

One: What a feast. I saw what they were eating.

Three: We all saw it.

Four: I've never seen so much food.

One: Do you suppose Levi will get some of it?

Two: Him? That crippled old man? He'll be tumbled out here in a minute, as rickety and slobbering as he ever was.

Three: No, no. He'll be healed. I know he will.

Two: Who do you think he is? Who do you think you are?

One: But you came. You helped carry him.

Four: You must believe.

Two: Believe? I only did what the old man wanted.

Three: Well, I came because they said this One, this Healer, is different.

26

Two: Oh yes, I've heard it all before. All of us have. The lame walk; the blind see; the deaf hear. And everyone will come to the table of the Lord.

(Two *proceeds to dance around them, parodying the words with his movements.*)

Two: "The eyes of the blind shall be opened, and the ears of the deaf unstopped; then shall the lame man leap like a hart, and the tongue of the dumb sing for joy. . . . And the ransomed of the Lord shall return, and come to Zion with singing; . . . they shall obtain joy and gladness, and sorrow and sighing shall flee away" (Isaiah 35:5-6, 10, RSV). Hogwash!

One: Yes, yes, that's what will happen.

Three: At least now, now, for Levi!

Four: He'll walk, and run, and dance.

Two: Take another look in the window, friends. See the table. Smell the meat, juicy and steaming. See, they pour the fine wines.

One: Ow, my stomach. My stomach.

Two: Yes, you ache now where all of us ache, in your belly. That's the only ache that is real and is never stopped. Look at the loaves of bread, warm from the ovens, thick-crusted, chewy, and sweet inside.

Three: Stop, stop. Don't say anymore. We shouldn't have come.

Four: It was wrong. It won't do any good.

(Two *picks up the "pack," which has been upstage a little. It is the red cloak wrapped around the bowl, the drum, the recorder, and the tambourine. As he speaks the next lines he gives the instruments to them.*)

Two: Here, my lords and ladies, here. The feast is for you: the feast of the holy mountain. Rarest fruits from all lands, for you, my lords, for you. Sweet delights from the hillsides of Kedar and Lebanon.

Tender meats from the flocks of Nabaoth, from the young calves of Bashan. And here, waters from all the earth. (*He pantomimes a bowl, scooping up "water" from the stream.*)

Water, distilled from the rivers of all the world, bubbling, cold, and pure: The Nile, the Jordan, the Chebar.

Here, beneath this tree, you are to feast and know goodness.

Ah yes, my lords and ladies. Yes, here we shall worship God. We shall see God's face, and God's name will be on our foreheads. And look, night shall be no more. We will need no lamp, nor sun, for the Lord God will be our light. And we shall reign forever and ever.

Ha, ha, ha, ha! (*He breaks out in raucous laughter.*)

ONE: No, no. Stop it. Stop it!

THREE: Stop. It's enough, enough.

FOUR: We're nothing, nothing. There's no good in us.

TWO: No good? No good? On the contrary, you poor wandering beggars, you're the ones who count, don't you know that? It's all yours: the whole Kingdom is yours, and it will never end. You dumb fools.

THREE: Stop it, stop it. It isn't for us.

ONE: You're making fun of us.

FOUR: Stop, stop. Why must you tell us this?

(Suddenly they all look to up right. They pantomime seeing the crowd come from "inside." Throughout the song, they "play up to" imaginary persons coming from the house up right, moving from up right to down left several times during the singing of the song. If possible they might also play to the audience in the front rows as also persons coming out of the house.)

TWO: Wait. Look. They're coming out.

ONE: Quick. Quick. It's time for our act.

FOUR: But what about Levi? He's still inside. In there.

THREE: We need him for the act.

TWO: Forget him. Quick.

(They all scramble to recover their instruments and get in place. TWO has the tambourine and throughout the song holds it out to the imaginary persons who come out of the house—or to the audience—as if requesting alms.)

ALL:
Come to the waters!
Come for the wine.
Buy without money.
Now is the time.

TWO:
No need to labor
Goodness to see.
Here is God's blessing,
Pardon that's free.

ALL:
Come to the waters!
Come for the wine.
Buy without money.
Now is the time.

FOUR:
    Rainfall from heaven.
      Snow with its cold.
    Grant us a token.
      Mercy's not sold.

ALL:
    Come to the waters!
      Come for the wine.
    Buy without money.
      Now is the time.

ONE:
    Joy and a blessing
      Keep you in peace.
    Share just a morsel,
      Crying will cease.

ALL:
    Come to the waters!
      Come for the wine.
    Buy without money.
      Now is the time.

THREE:
    Mountains are singing,
      Trees clap their hands,
    Up comes the cypress,
      Sign for all lands.

ALL:
    Come to the waters!
      Come for the wine.
    Buy without money.
      Now is the time.

(The crowd—the banqueters—have passed by, spurning the Players.)

THREE: Not a cent.

ONE: Not a cent!

FOUR: They didn't even see us.

TWO: We're losing our touch, friends. We need a refresher course.

THREE: Look, here comes Levi. (LEVI *begins to enter from up right.*)

ONE: And he still limps. He can't walk.

FOUR: He won't be dancing.

(LEVI *enters. He leans on his staff, walking with difficulty.*)

ONE: How was it?

THREE: What happened? *(As they crowd around him)*

TWO: We thought they'd eaten you for supper.

ONE: Are you cured?

FOUR: Is it better?

THREE: What did he say to you?

TWO: Let's see you walk, old boy. Come on. Do a dance for us.

(They step back from him a little. He moves to them, too quickly, and falls to the ground. They run to him.)

ONE: It's no better.

THREE: Yes it is. It is. Anyone can fall.

FOUR: You ought to know, just tell him.

TWO *(suddenly softening toward him):* Here, we'll help you. Maybe, maybe you are better.

LEVI *(as he is pulled up):* You're to come in. You're invited, all of you.

THREE: What are you talking about? Come on. We've got to get away.

FOUR: Those people, they'll tell the police. We'll be locked up.

TWO: Locked up again. Well, at least it's a free meal.

ONE: We've got to get away. Come on. You can walk a little. And we'll carry you again. We can do it.

FOUR: Someday we'll find another healer—who will really heal you.

LEVI: It doesn't matter, it doesn't matter. Don't you understand? You're invited. He wants you to join Him, to eat with Him.

THREE: What are you talking about? What do you mean? Us, in there?

TWO: He's gone mad. Seeing all that food did it.

ONE: And the excitement, falling through the roof.

FOUR: That poor little tree, Levi.

ONE: We could never climb it again.

30

LEVI: We don't have to go in through the roof, not anymore. He told me . . . He told me, it's all right. I don't need to worry about it, about me, about the past. All that is over. He put His arm around me. He washed the dust from my feet. He took the bowl, the water, himself and He washed my feet. Then I sat next to Him. And it's all right. And I'm to tell you. Yes, I must tell you. You don't have to worry anymore. Any of you. Joy and blessing, they're yours. I'm to tell you.

THREE: What are you saying, Levi? What do you mean?

FOUR: What about your leg that won't move, and your arm?

LEVI: I tell you, that doesn't matter. He said it, and I believe it now. And you will too. Come on, come on. The feast is for you. It's yours. Wine and water, milk and bread.

FOUR: What about the others?

LEVI: They're gone. They all left. They didn't like it when He looked at me and asked me to sit beside Him. They were afraid. So they left. He told me to come and get you.

THREE: I am hungry.

ONE: The act didn't go well.

FOUR: They wouldn't give us a cent.

TWO: We needed you, Levi. That leg of yours always gets to them. The act didn't work at all.

LEVI: There's food here, for you. And more than that: Everything in the past is over. It's all right. You're invited. We're all invited, and we always have been. That's what He said. And now, I'm to tell you.

ONE: Me? But does He know about me? You know, all of you, you know what I've been.

THREE: I am hungry. But they won't let me in . . . only by the backdoor and then only for an instant.

TWO: The feast is for us? It can't be. I'm cursed. A crust of bread is all I deserve.

FOUR: But they hear me yelling, and screaming, and they spit on me.

LEVI: He sees. He knows. And He says to come, to come to the feast.

ONE: But me? My stumbling, my complaining, no one ever . . . *(He falls to his knees.)*

THREE: They call me names. I'm nothing, nothing. *(Falls to her knees)*

TWO: I've refused to hope; doubted, again and again. *(Falls to his knees)*

FOUR: No one listens to me, so I yell, and I hurt them, always. *(Falls to her knees)*

LEVI: O Lord, forgive us. *(He goes to his knees.)*

(The organist begins to play the hymn as they all are still praying.)

The Betrothal

by Teresa Burleson

Characters:
> AMOS
> HOSEA

Scene I

(At the prophet HOSEA's *home shortly before his wedding.)*

HOSEA: I heard a word from Yahweh, Amos.

AMOS: Hosea, are you sure it was Him? Or your own deluded fancy? Do you know what kind of girl she is? Can't you see? Haven't you heard what people are saying about her?

HOSEA: I know that she is lovely. She is like fire. She brings laughter to a life that knew no laughter. I need her, Amos. I need her laughter.

AMOS: You're infatuated!

HOSEA: Yes, I'm infatuated, and I'm commanded by Yahweh to take her as my wife.

AMOS: Even knowing what she is?

HOSEA: Yes, even knowing what she is.

AMOS: May Yahweh help you, my brother. You will need it.

Scene II

*(*HOSEA's *home seven years later.* AMOS *is playing with* HOSEA's *little boy Jezreel.)*

AMOS: What a sturdy lad! How he has grown. How much he looks like you, my friend.

HOSEA: Yes, the resemblance is plain. I wish I could say the same about his sisters.

AMOS: What do you mean?

HOSEA: I mean you were right about Gomer. The most beautiful thing in my life has proved to be the most false. She sought other beds, and neither of the girls are mine.

AMOS: She should be stoned! And your hand should throw the first stone.

HOSEA: Could I stone my bride, my love, the mother of my son?

AMOS: Where is she now?

HOSEA: I do not know. As soon as the baby was weaned she left me. My mother cares for the little ones.

AMOS: This is horrible! I have always believed God to be just. If He is not just, then He is not God. This is my faith. This is the message I preach. But now He tells you to marry a harlot and she betrays you and you are left with three motherless children. This is not just. How could He allow such a thing?

HOSEA: I am a symbol, Amos. You of all people should know how He loves to use symbols. How He will go to any length to make a point. Can't you see Israel betraying Him the very same way Gomer betrayed me?

AMOS: Yes, I see what you mean. We prophets are the visual aids He uses to teach His lessons. But it hurts me to see what it's done to you. We are not mere puppets for Him to toy with.

HOSEA: Not puppets, Amos, but willing instruments. Oh, Amos, you know what it is to be used by Him. You of all people know that there is nothing higher than to be used by Him. Well, He is using me to demonstrate how He loves His wanton bride, Israel.

AMOS: But what right does He have to ask you to bear such pain?

HOSEA: Have you forgotten He is the Creator? We are but creatures. He is God, and we are His to do with as He wills. Besides, He feels the same pain I do. He asks me to do nothing He has not already done.

AMOS: I am beginning to see that there is far more to God than justice. Far more.

HOSEA: And now I must complete the allegory.

AMOS: What do you mean?

HOSEA: I must buy her back.

AMOS: Buy her back! You can't mean it, Hosea.

HOSEA: Yes, I am to take her back as my wife.

AMOS: But what if she hasn't changed? What if she never changes? She may play the wanton again and again.

HOSEA: I know. That is the risk I must take. That is the risk God keeps taking with every one of us. You see, Amos, there is a little Gomer in all of us. We keep playing the wanton. And He still takes us back. He still calls us His beloved.

Zack

by Kevin C. Kato

Characters:

NARRATOR
ZACK: chief tax collector of Jericho
OBADIAH: a young tax collector-in-training
VERA: Zack's wife
RUTH: Zack's teenage daughter
BARTHOLOMEW: Zack's young son
3 VOICES: tax protestors
VOICE OF JESUS

Setting:

Upper room of Zack's house, day

Scene:

Interior of an upper room of a house circa the time of Christ. A large window, through which a stout tree trunk with several large branches can be seen, is situated in the upstage center wall. Stage left is a desk with many money bags, marked with dollar signs, on top of and around it. A portrait of a Roman emperor is mounted on the wall behind the desk. Hanging next to it is a framed certificate. The room is full of pretentious furniture, knickknacks, and tapestries from different historical periods. Enter NARRATOR wearing a Roman toga and carrying a scroll.

NARRATOR *(unrolling the scroll; enunciating crisply):* Zack was a wee, little man, and a wee, little man was he. He was chief of all the tax collectors and charged the people an exorbitant fee.

(Exit NARRATOR as ZACK, a short, middle-aged man, and his assistant tax collector-in-training, OBADIAH, enter. ZACK and OBADIAH are both wearing Roman togas. ZACK has an unlit cigar clenched between his teeth and is carrying a bulky briefcase. OBADIAH, a young man fresh out of tax collecting school, is trailing behind carrying a clipboard in one hand with a folder bulging with papers and receipts tucked under one arm, and in the other hand, a large bag of money.)

OBADIAH *(holding up the bag of money):* What do you want me to do with all the tax money, Boss?

ZACK *(pointing with his cigar):* Just put it over there with the rest of the loot.

(OBADIAH *puts the bag of money down with a clink.* ZACK *sets his briefcase down and sits down in the chair behind the desk and props up his feet on top of the desk.*)

ZACK *(stretching):* It's been quite a *taxing* day!

OBADIAH *(politely laughing at the pun):* It sure has been, Boss.

ZACK: What percentage did we end up getting off that widow?

OBADIAH *(checking his clipboard):* Checking the short list, Boss.

ZACK *(angrily):* What did I hear you say?

OBADIAH *(hastily):* I mean the *brief* list, Boss.

ZACK: Much better. Go on.

OBADIAH: Let's see . . . we collected 8 shekels from her monthly widow's pension of 10 shekels . . . 80 percent of her income was taxed, Boss.

ZACK: Excellent! Did you see what a fuss she made when we tried to collect? *(Scornfully)* Pretending she was just a poor widow.

OBADIAH: Yes, but Boss, shouldn't you have gone a little easier on her? After all, she is your mother.

ZACK: Don't worry. Believe me, she's got plenty of money stashed away in long-term CDs. Besides, taxation is an inalienable right of every man, woman, and child!

(There is the sound of glass breaking as a rock comes flying through the window. ZACK *hurriedly gets up and goes over to the window and throws open the sash.* VOICES *from below can be heard.)*

VOICES *(chanting together):* No taxation without representation!

ZACK: You'll hear from my lawyers about this!

(ZACK *slams the window shut and goes back to his desk.)*

ZACK *(angrily):* Those liberal tax protesters. I wish the emperor would round them all up and feed them to the lions. Don't they realize taxes are what make the world go around?

OBADIAH: But, Boss, they're probably upset because you tax 70 percent of their income.

ZACK *(defensively):* Fifty percent goes to Rome, 20 percent goes to me. I have to make a living, too, you know. I have a wife and two kids to support—one who will soon be in college.

OBADIAH *(apologetically):* Sorry, Boss. I don't know what I was thinking.

ZACK: Obadiah, stick with me and I'll teach you everything there is to know about the fine art of tax collecting. If you work hard enough, you, too, may someday be named "Tax Collector of the Year." *(Points with his cigar to the certificate hanging on the wall)*

*(*OBADIAH *moves to take a closer look at the certificate.)*

OBADIAH *(awed):* Tax Collector of the Year!

ZACK: Now get out there and collect those taxes! We still haven't collected from the orphanage.

OBADIAH: Yes, sir. This time I'll be careful. I remember last year the director short-changed us.

ZACK *(angrily):* What did I hear you say?

OBADIAH *(frightened):* Er . . . I mean he didn't pay us in full. I'd better get going.

(Exit OBADIAH *as* ZACK *sits back down and props his feet back up on his desk. Enter* VERA, RUTH, *and* BARTHOLOMEW.)

VERA: Get your feet off the furniture right now!

ZACK *(sitting up immediately):* Vera! I thought you and the children had gone to the market.

VERA: We just got back. And get rid of that foul-smelling cigar. You know it's bad for the children's health.

ZACK *(meekly):* Yes, Dear. *(He throws the cigar into the trash can.)*

VERA: Just look at this place! The maid was just here yesterday, and you wouldn't know it. Supper will be ready in an hour, and I want this mess cleaned up before then.

ZACK *(with a sigh):* Yes, Dear.

VERA *(sweetly to the children):* Ruth, Bartholomew, tell your father how school was today *(tersely to* ZACK), since your father was too busy to ask.

ZACK: How was school today?

RUTH *(chewing bubble gum):* Fine.

BART: Fine.

ZACK: And what did you learn in school today, Ruth?

RUTH: Stuff.

ZACK: And you, Bart?

BART: We had to tell the class what our fathers did for a living.

ZACK *(his pride aroused):* Oh, and what did you tell them?

BART: I told them that you were the chief tax collector for the entire district of Jericho.

ZACK *(pleased):* Well said, Son!

BART: Father, what's a *(stumbling over the word)* swindler?

ZACK: What!?

BART *(innocently):* A swindler. One of the other kids called you that after I told them what you did for a living.

VERA: Come along, children, your father has had a very long day. We need to let him rest a little before dinner.

(RUTH and BART exit.)

ZACK *(indignant):* A swindler! The nerve of that child. First thing tomorrow morning, I'm going to the principal and demand an apology, and if the principal doesn't do anything about it, I'll just raise the school's taxes!

VERA *(soothingly):* Now, now, Dear. Don't let it upset you so. You'll feel better after eating supper. *(She kisses ZACK on the forehead.)*

(Exit VERA. ZACK walks aimlessly around the room. As he passes by the window, VOICES outside can be heard again.)

VOICES *(together):* No taxation without representation!

(ZACK angrily throws open the window.)

ZACK *(angrily):* Shut up!

(He slams the window shut and continues to walk aimlessly around the room.)

ZACK *(reflectively):* You know, I always thought that if I were only rich, I'd be happy. I have all this money, all these things, but to tell the truth, I'm still not happy. There's got to be more to life than what a man possesses. If you get right down to it, the only thing that really matters to me is my family. What was it my grandfather used to always say to us? "What does it profit a man if he gains the whole world but loses his soul?" *(As if a light bulb comes on in his head)* That's me! I've gained the whole world but lost my soul! *(In anguish)* What am I to do?

(ZACK sits down with his head in his hands. Excited VOICES can be heard outside the window.)

VOICE 1: Look! Jesus is coming!

VOICE 2: Jesus is coming!

VOICE 3: Jesus, the Messiah, is coming!

(ZACK *lifts his head and listens.*)

ZACK: Jesus is coming? *(Gets up)* I must see Him. He's the only one who can help me.

(ZACK *hurriedly exits. Through the window, we can see* ZACK *climbing the tree until he is out of sight. Enter* VERA, RUTH, BART, *and* OBADIAH. *They all hurry over to the window.*)

VERA *(calling out the window):* Zack, what in the world are you doing climbing a tree at your age? Come down right now! What will the neighbors think?

ZACK *(from the tree):* I can't, dear. I must see Jesus.

RUTH *(turning away from the window):* Great, we'll be the laughingstock at school tomorrow.

BART *(also turning away from the window):* Maybe we can quietly move to Bethany.

VERA: I knew he was long overdue for a vacation. He's gone completely out of his mind! Obadiah!

OBADIAH: Yes, ma'am?

VERA: Go out there and get him down.

OBADIAH: Yes, ma'am. *(Exits)*

VOICE 1: Jesus is coming!

VOICE 2: Look! There He is!

VOICE 3: Lord! Lord!

VOICE OF JESUS: Zack, come down immediately. Today I must stay at your house.

ZACK: Yes, Lord. Vera, quick, set another place for dinner!

VERA: Hurry, children, you've heard your father. Jesus is coming to our house.

(*Exit* VERA, RUTH, *and* BART. *Enter* NARRATOR.)

NARRATOR *(reading from a scroll):* Yes, Zack was a wee, little man, and wee, little man was he. One day he met the Lord Jesus Christ, and he and his household were set free.

The Elevator

by Sara Pasiciel

Characters:

ROBERTSON JONES: senior executive, harried, self-important

STANLEY PRUITT: junior executive, anxious to please, but self-motivated—a "yuppie"

SUSAN DAVIS: also a young professional, a "manager" used to being listened to; organized, efficient, impatient

ELEANOR WINDOM: middle-aged, paying a visit to her son, the lawyer; laden with packages from a shopping trip, she is twitty and excitable, with a solid core of common sense

BEN: a derelict of indeterminate age, he has come into the building to keep warm, finds the elevator music soothing

Setting:

The action of the play takes place within an imagined confined space of approximately 5' x 5'. There are no stage props, but the actors should be very conscious of the "walls," and a few hand props and minimal costume suggestions would be helpful (e.g., packages, briefcases, ties for the men, hat for ELEANOR, etc.).

The play opens with BEN already on the elevator, slouched against the rear "wall." As each character gets on the elevator, we "see" the elevator stop, the doors open, and the characters acknowledge each other's presence with appropriate nods, clearing of throats, etc. All characters enter from stage left or stage right, stand with backs to the audience as they "wait" for the elevator, then turn to face the front of the elevator, toward the audience, as they enter the elevator.

(ROBERTSON *enters elevator, pushes button, checks watch, indicates nonverbal displeasure at* BEN's *presence.*)

BEN: Mornin'. Nice up here on the top floor, ain't it?

ROBERTSON: Hmmph.

(STANLEY *enters, recognizes* ROBERTSON, *and reacts.*)

STANLEY: Good morning, sir! Is your day going well?

ROBERTSON: Oh, yes. Thompson, is it?

STANLEY: Pruitt, sir.

ROBERTSON: Of course—from processing.

40

STANLEY: Accounting, sir.

ROBERTSON: Hmmmph.

(ELEANOR *enters, smiles, nods, and jockeys for position with packages in hand.*)

ELEANOR: Would you please punch the main floor button for me? My hands are so full. Oh, of course. I guess most of us going down would be going to the main floor. I get so nervous when I visit my son in this huge office building . . .

(ELEANOR *notices that the others are ignoring her—except* BEN, *who just shakes his head. She closes her mouth tightly, faces front.*)

(SUSAN *enters, checks elevator panel, pushes button anyway, folds her arms, and faces front.*)

(*After a few seconds, characters indicate a jolt—the elevator has stopped. All look at the panel and then at each other.* ROBERTSON *begins pushing buttons.*)

SUSAN: What's wrong? This is so typical . . . brand-new office building, state-of-the-art technology . . . what's wrong?

ROBERTSON: Obviously we have stopped at an unintended point, but I'm sure there's no need to worry.

ELEANOR: It should start up again soon, shouldn't it? I mean, I dream about something like this happening, but you never think it's really going to happen to you. (*Once again quelled by glances from others*)

STANLEY: Maybe we should try the phone, sir. (*He is beginning to look nervous, jittery.*)

ROBERTSON: I think it's likely that the problem is being solved already, but I will certainly see if I can contact . . . Hello, hello . . . can you hear me? Nothing—there seems to be a rather complete breakdown. In fact, I hear no sound from anywhere—most unusual.

(BEN *sits down, settles for long wait.*)

BEN: Anyone bring a sandwich?

(*The others notice him, react, move away a bit, but find that if they move away from* BEN, *they are closer to each other. At this point, try to keep equal space between all of them.*)

SUSAN: Well, let me try. (*Moves over in front of panel*) Sometimes if you just read the directions . . . nothing! I have an appointment in 10 minutes, an urgent appointment!

STANLEY: Can't we do something? We have to get out of here. I have to get out of here. I'm severely claustrophobic. We've got to do something, sir.

ROBERTSON: We must just assume that somebody is realizing that there is a problem and is beginning to work at rectifying the situation. There's no need for panic.

STANLEY: No, sir. *(Waits a beat)* How long should we wait before we panic, sir?

SUSAN *(to* ELEANOR*)*: Just my luck. I get stuck on an elevator in the big city, and I meet a wimp and a bum.

ELEANOR: Well, maybe we should just relax and enjoy our time together!

(Appropriate reactions from others)

ELEANOR *(to* BEN*)*: May I just set my packages down here by your feet? I bought some pots and pans at the Bay sale and they're getting a bit heavy.

BEN: It's a free country, lady.

ELEANOR: Now! My name is Eleanor Windom, and I was just visiting my son—he's a lawyer on the 19th floor. It's nice to meet you, Miss . . .

SUSAN: Ms.; Susan Davis *(still stiff),* I'm office manager at The Mutual.

STANLEY: This is all very nice, but aren't you the least little bit worried about getting out of here? Should we try the phone again, sir? Maybe if I tried . . .

ROBERTSON *(will not easily give up this space again):* I'm sure that you cannot . . . hello, hello? Still nothing. Pull yourself together, Thompson.

STANLEY: Pruitt. I'll try, sir. It's just that I can't help being aware that we're suspended by a very thin coil of wire about 15 floors above a very hard bottom of this narrow, little, dark hole . . .

ROBERTSON: Try not to fall apart, young man. There isn't a great deal we can do. *(Somewhat sarcastically)* Unless you have a suggestion . . .

STANLEY: Yes sir, I do . . . HELP!

SUSAN: Can you believe it?

STANLEY: HELP! HELP! *(Continues to cry out at intervals)*

ROBERTSON: Young man . . .

ELEANOR *(with hands over ears):* It really can't do any good.

BEN: America's future.

ROBERTSON: That's really quite enough. I would expect my employees to show a bit of grace under pressure, Thompson.

STANLEY *(still breathing heavily):* That's Pruitt, sir.

ROBERTSON: Yes, yes. I'm Robertson Jones. As it happens, I own this building, and I know that the finest and best efforts will be made to correct this problem and . . .

BEN: Well, what do you know. *(Gets to feet, approaches* ROBERTSON *with hand out for handshake)* Allow me to thank you for your hospitality during these cold winter months.

ROBERTSON: But there's no way . . .

BEN: Just because a man ain't got no money don't mean he ain't got some sense. There are always ways to find a warm place.

ELEANOR: Why, you poor man. Do you mean you have no place to live?

SUSAN: From the odor, I'd say he's been living here for the past three years!

ELEANOR: But that's awful! I had no idea!

STANLEY: What does all of this have to do with anything? Is this going to get us out of here? How are we going to get out of here!

SUSAN: Look, don't panic, Thompson.

STANLEY: Pruitt! Stanley Pruitt!

SUSAN: Whatever. We can handle this, you know. We're well-educated, well-prepared, highly trained individuals. Surely between us we can, if not solve our dilemma, at least handle it while we're in it.

ROBERTSON: Well said, Miss, um, Ms. Davis. Which company did you say you work for?

ELEANOR *(looking up):* Isn't there usually some kind of little door . . . ?

ROBERTSON: Of course!

STANLEY *(jumping up):* I'll try, I'll try!

SUSAN: You idiot!

BEN: Fasten your seat belts for immediate landing.

ELEANOR: Do you think you should . . . ?

ROBERTSON *(grabbing* STANLEY*)*: Stop and think, Thomp . . . Pruitt! It's precarious enough as it is!

(STANLEY *realizing what he has done, is horrified.)*

ROBERTSON: Here, Ms. Davis—climb up and see if it will budge.

(ROBERTSON *and the still shaking* STANLEY *make a bridge for* SUSAN *to climb.* SUSAN *pushes against the ceiling but cannot make any headway.)*

SUSAN: No, it's tight. Doesn't seem to even be a door here. It's sealed pretty well as far as I can see.

(BEN *begins tapping on the floor.)*

BEN: Anyone know Morse code? All I remember is SOS.

STANLEY: That's good! That's enough! That's what we need! Keep tapping! *(The tapping continues as the lights dim.)*

(*Blackout. During this change of scene, characters adjust clothing, position, otherwise indicate the passage of time.* BEN *is still feebly and occasionally tapping—stops after first line.)*

STANLEY: What time is it now, sir?

ROBERTSON: It's five o'clock.

STANLEY: They're not going to fix it, are they? They would have fixed it long ago if they could. *(He is weary and resigned now, rather than panic-stricken, but still frightened.)* They should have had us out of here hours ago!

ELEANOR: Oh, do you think he's right?

ROBERTSON: That's preposterous. Of course they're going to fix it. It's just a matter of finding out what the problem is. This is a highly sophisticated system, but new. It may take some trial and error . . .

SUSAN: Error!

STANLEY: Do you know what error means when you're hanging in an elevator?

ROBERTSON: Unfortunate choice of words. Surely they'll be able to . . .

BEN: Hey, lady, you got any more of that candy?

ELEANOR: No, it's all gone . . . and the gum . . . and the cheese left over from my lunch.

BEN: Don't any of you carry food in those little suitcases?

SUSAN: I will from now on!

STANLEY: If there is a now on . . .

ROBERTSON: Shhh! I hear some . . . *(all are quiet, listening).* Yes, they've got the machinery working.

(There is a sudden hard jolt—all characters shift to one side—then nothing.)

STANLEY: I knew it! This is it, isn't it? HELP! HELP!

ROBERTSON: Please! We all want to get out of here. . . . *(Thoughtfully)* I have a wife and three children.

ELEANOR *(who has been getting calmer and more composed):* I've been thinking about my family too.

SUSAN: I haven't had a chance to have a family yet.

BEN: Families ain't all they're cracked up to be, y'know.

STANLEY: Families, schmamilies, I DON'T WANT TO DIE!

(There is a sudden shocked silence as all realize that this is a possibility.)

ELEANOR: We've tried everything else. Would you let me pray for you?

STANLEY: Good idea. I'm too panicked to get in touch with my mantra.

SUSAN: You don't mean that, do you?

ELEANOR: No. I'm a Christian; my faith is in God and in His Son, Jesus Christ.

BEN: Yeah, I know Christians. They give me soup and a place to stay sometimes.

ROBERTSON: I'm sure none of us would be offended at this point at any attempt to provide help.

ELEANOR: Lord, we've come to the end of our own strength and knowledge. We are in Your hands, and we pray that You will provide help in some way. But if we are not rescued, we pray for Your grace and Your forgiveness as we come to the end of our lives on this earth.

STANLEY: But you see, I can't die . . . I'm not ready to die.

SUSAN: For the first time, I agree with you.

BEN: It can't be worse than what I've got here.

ELEANOR: It could be so much better!

BEN: There?

ELEANOR: And here.

(There is a startling, unexpected sound of a buzzer.)

STANLEY: What's that?

SUSAN: It's the phone, the phone!

(All reach for it, ROBERTSON *picks it up.)*

ROBERTSON: Yes, yes . . . yes, we're here, we're all fine. No there are five of us . . . Susan Davis, Stan Pruitt, Eleanor Windom, and Ben . . . uh, Ben doesn't work in the building. Yes, yes, we'll keep the line open . . . yes, we'll be ready! *(Puts phone down)* Thank God.

ELEANOR: Yes, I think that is entirely appropriate.

STANLEY: When? How soon do we get out of here?

ROBERTSON: They're sending men down the elevator shaft with a power saw. Apparently our technology broke down completely and we have to rely on old-fashioned muscle!

SUSAN *(beginning to pull herself together):* Well! A few moments of weakness there, but it looks as though everything is going to be just fine and back to normal. It'll take a few days to get my schedule organized again . . .

STANLEY: I will never get on an elevator again. I will never get on an elevator . . .

BEN: And to think I used to like elevator music . . .

SUSAN: You mean . . .

BEN: Sure, why else would I be riding up and down an elevator?

ROBERTSON: Mrs. Windom . . .

ELEANOR: Eleanor, please.

ROBERTSON: Eleanor, may my wife and I pay you a visit within the next few days? You reminded me of some questions I have and some answers I should be looking for.

STANLEY: Do you mean that God stuff, . . . sir? I've got a great guru I'd be glad to put you in touch with.

ROBERTSON: Pruitt, I'm afraid you're headed in the wrong direction.

STANLEY: Yes, sir. *(Puzzled)* Does this mean I've lost my job?

ROBERTSON: No, Pruitt. I just hope you haven't lost your way.

BEN: Here's your packages, lady.

ELEANOR: And where will you go, Ben?

BEN: I think I'll go back to that place with the Christians.

ELEANOR: For soup?

BEN *(sheepishly):* That too.

ELEANOR: Susan, I hope you find what you're looking for.

SUSAN: I will. It's in the five-year plan.

ELEANOR: Which almost ended today. Oh! Here they come!

(Characters begin to "get ready" for the rescue—STANLEY and SUSAN face front, as at the beginning of the play; BEN is standing looking up for his rescuers; ELEANOR and ROBERTSON smiling at each other. Blackout.)

Born Blind

A Monologue

by John G. Papanikolas

Props:

A single desk with a chair

A white cane rests on the chair

Four spotlights or bright directional lamps (may or may not be seen by the audience)

A hidden box of large wooden matches

(A man is sitting in the chair. He wears a trench coat and hat. The stage and auditorium are dark. Suddenly a bright light, from one of the four lamps, flashes in his face. He shields his eyes from the glare by crossing his hands over his face. He speaks.)

That light is blinding me.

(Pause)

Besides, I already *told* you what happened. Is it a crime to see?

(Longer pause as his inquisitors berate him)

OK! OK! I'm not trying to be smart. I just don't understand this.

(Longer pause)

Glasses? . . . What glasses? I never *owned* any glasses. They wouldn't have helped me anyway. Everything was black before He saw me.

(Pause. He looks down and slowly shakes his head in disbelief and frustration at the continued questioning.)

(Slowly at first)

No, I can't *tell* you how He did it. Look, I'm no rocket scientist. He saw me. He put mud on my eyes. I washed. And as I was walking back, blue skies shot into sight—yellow flowers, green grass, tall trees. I could almost *smell* the color green. You see what I mean?

He was there. He smiled. He left. Let's not make a federal case out of this.

(Second light flashes on. He cringes away from it, again shielding his eyes, and backs out of his chair, standing.)

Well, would you feel any better if I told you He dropped out of a spaceship and blasted me twice in each eye with laser guns?

(He looks up, thinking.)

48

No . . . No . . . A team of surgeons—that's it—surgeons and six nurses tackled me to the ground. They slapped mud packs on my eyes, and—voilà!—here I am! *(He extends his arms wide—straight out like a "T.")*

(Pause. He slowly drops his arms to his sides and hangs his head as he hears his accusers rebuke him.)

(Quietly. Dejected.)

OK, I'm joking—I'm *joking*. Can't you take a joke? . . . I tell you again, I don't *know* how He did it.

(Long pause)

Oh . . . this? *(He looks at the white cane and then picks it up.)* I carry it around to remind me how it was before He saw me. Sometimes I use it to knock apples off high limbs. I really like the *green* ones.

See those paint chips? *(He points to the tip.)* It's rapped a lot of street curbs.

(He hits it three times on the ground, confident and smiling, lost in thought.)

(Third light flashes on. His smile turns to surprise and shock. Talking quickly.)

Look, I never said I was *perfect*. Sure, I sin. I sip a little wine once in a while. I might peek at the lingerie ads in the newspaper.

But, I wouldn't say I was "born" in sin.

(He pauses to think.)

Actually, I was born in Milwaukee.

(He snickers at his little joke, but then flinches, expecting a rebuke. None comes and he catches himself, speaking fearfully, rapidly.)

Look, Mom and Dad could tell you where I was born. They could tell you all about my birth—they were there. Ask them!

(Pause)

(Quietly)

. . . They said to ask me? . . . Well, I don't think He's a sinner. I don't know what He is, but I don't think He's a sinner. Look, I was born blind and now I can see—that's about all I know.

(Pause)

I *told* you—No, I don't think He's a sinner. You keep asking me the same questions, again and again. Do you think if you keep hearing me talk, you'll follow Him too?

(Fourth light flashes on. He covers his eyes with his fingers again.)

Boy, you guys are touchy! Lighten up a bit! . . . It makes sense, doesn't it? Besides, I told you all I know. He was there. I could see. He left. Don't you see?

Look, if you want to know more about Him, you should ask someone else. Lots of people know about Him, really . . .

(He starts slowly and then speaks more and more rapidly as he says the following.)

. . . Why, just the other day I heard about a little girl who died, and He just touched her, and, well . . . and then there was the lady who was bleeding and *she* touched *Him*. Oh, and Lazarus. I'm sure you've heard about Lazarus! And the little boy who kept falling into the fire, but no one could help him. Then there was that crazy man who cut himself on the rocks, and a man with a withered hand, and the little girl with a fever, and the soldier's servant who was almost dead, and that cripple by the pool who couldn't get in, and—

(Abruptly—in midsentence—all lights in the house shut off. Ten to 20 seconds of darkness and silence pass. The man, standing alone on the stage, strikes a single wooden match. He holds it near his chin, peering up. He puts his hands together in prayer. He then gently blows it out.)

The Judgment

A Monologue

by Martha Bolton

Props:

A bright light coming from offstage or from another position equally hidden from view. The only thing evident to the audience should be the light's reflection.

(Someone offstage announces: "The life of JERROD WADE SIMMONS is hereby revealed for judgment.")

(JERROD WADE SIMMONS *approaches the light. Monologue begins.)*

Your Holiness, I am humbled in Your presence. You are mighty and fair; and Your judgments are final. I will not appeal Your decision, for You know my life. You know who I am.

(Pacing) I have watched the infinite line of Your creation go before You with fear and trembling. One by one they have nervously stood before Your bejeweled throne and awaited Your salutation. Would the door to paradise be opened by Your words, "Welcome home," or would they be cursed with the title of "stranger," and damned to an everlasting hell?

So many have already been turned away. I have heard their screams of anguish. They have echoed throughout the Holy City and tormented those of us awaiting our own judgment. Each time You have spoken those words, "Depart from Me, I never knew you," it was as if You were sentencing me. I have tasted eternal death even before my name was called.

I have watched the loved ones of those condemned scream and beg for mercy, but Your mercy has expired. We have all earned our wages now being issued.

(Pause) In Your judgment, Sir, I know that You will consider all the good I did for mankind while on earth. I confess I failed to accept Your Son, Jesus. I'm sure You know that already, but in all due respect, Sir, You didn't make it very easy for us to believe. You let us deny His deity without immediate consequence. You let us crucify Him without angelic interference. You even let us mock Your own existence without the sun falling down from the sky. Why didn't You force us to believe? Why didn't You program us to serve You? The decision of eternity was too important to have trusted to freewill agents.

You asked us to believe in Someone whom we had never met, Someone who loved us before we were even born, and gave His life that we might live forever. Sir, You have to realize how difficult that was to do on earth. But now I am a believer—a true believer. And I know there are many more waiting in line, so I'll be brief, but Your Holiness, I beg You to reconsider my life and grant me amnesty from Your judgment. I can see heaven is everything You promised it would be, and I know hell is everyting You warned it would be. Grant me passage through Your gates of pearl, and I will sing Your songs of praise forever.

(Pause) Sir, You keep silent. Surely, You cannot overlook all the good I've done. You know my résumé. I've fed Your poor. I've helped Your needy. If it wasn't for me and donations, many of Your own servants would have gone hungry. You see, You needed me then and I helped You. Now You can help me in return. Judge me by my charities and not by Your law. Review my record, and You will know who I am. I await Your welcome.

(Voice from offstage calls next person in line after brief pause: WILLIAM GARY SLATER. *Next person in line comes on stage and walks toward the light, but stops when* JERROD *addresses him.)*

Wait! *(Motions for next person to hold back)* Your Honor, You're sending me away, aren't You? You can't do that! You don't understand. You can't do this to *me!* What about my family? They've already passed through Your gates! You can't separate us for eternity! You can't do this to me, I say! You don't know who I am! You can't damn me to everlasting hell after all I've done for You! Where's Your love? Where's Your great forgiveness?

(Next person in line steps forward a little more toward the light. JERROD *begins to back off a little, but keeps talking.)*

You are a God of judgment! You are not a God of life anymore! Only a God of judgment could send His creation to eternal damnation!

(As if replying to God) It's the law? Curse the law! Erase our sins now; You have the power. It can't be too late. Give us just one more chance. Open heaven's gates and let us all pass through. We will worship You. We will kiss Your holy hands and praise You forever!

(Anxious pause, waiting for a response) Dear God, say something! Your silence is cold and judging. Love me once again! You sent Your Son to die for me; You can't turn Your back on me now. Look at me through the eyes of grace.

(Next person in line, WILLIAM GARY SLATER, *approaches light as if there was a gesture from God to do so.* JERROD *backs off, but as he is leaving the stage, he's crying and screaming . . .)*

You can't do this to me! Don't You know who I am? Don't You even know my name?

(To WILLIAM GARY SLATER) He doesn't know who I am! *(As he is leaving stage in anguish)* He doesn't even know who I am!

(While you can still hear speaker crying in agony offstage, WILLIAM GARY SLATER *positions himself before the light. Voice from offstage says:* "The life of WILLIAM GARY SLATER is now revealed for judgment." *Blackout.)*